God

RABBI RAMI
GUIDE TO

God

--- Roadside Assistance for the Spiritual Traveler ---

Spirituality
&Health
BOOKS

Rabbi Rami Guide to God:
Roadside Assistance for the Spiritual Traveler
By Rami Shapiro

© 2011 Rami Shapiro

425 Boardman Street, Suite C
Traverse City, MI 49684
www.spiritualityhealthbooks.com

Printed in Canada.

Cover and interior design by Sandra Salamony

Cataloging-in-Publication data for this book is available
upon request.

978-0-9818708-4-7
10 9 8 7 6 5 4 3 2 1

CONTENTS

PREFACE

DO YOU BELIEVE IN GOD? Wait a moment before you answer. It's too easy to say "yes" or "no" to this question, and the question itself is vague to the point of being meaningless. Before you can answer "yes" or "no" to a belief in God, you have to know just what it is the questioner means by the word *God*.

For example, if you ask practicing Jews, Christians, and Muslims if they believe in God, chances are most of them will say, "yes." But if you then ask them, "Do you believe in God, a singular divine being who yet embraces three persons: Father, Son, and Holy Spirit?" the very same Jews and Muslims who affirmed a belief in God just a moment ago, suddenly will stand with the atheists and declare their nonbelief in this God.

In other words, the word *God* in and of itself tells us nothing, and saying one believes or disbelieves in God is equally meaningless. Before you can affirm or deny a belief in God, you have to define the term. And when you do, things get so much more complicated.

I dislike complication. While I find the world to be marvelously complex, complication is something else. Complication arises not from the nature of the world, but from the nature of the human mind seeking to define the world. Returning to the example of the Trinity, for example, it doesn't take long to discover that this doctrine, while central to most of Christianity, is nearly impossible to define or explain. Why is God one–in–three? How is God one–in–three? What is the relationship between the Father, Son, and Holy Spirit? Are they equal, or is God the Father somehow more than God the Son or the Holy Spirit? Did one come before the others? Trinitarians believe that the Son is "begotten" by the Father. Does that mean the Father is greater than the Son? And does the Spirit proceed from the Father alone, as Orthodox Christians insist, or from the Father and the Son together as Catholics insist?

These are serious arguments. Indeed, this last was one of the reasons the Christian world split into Roman Catholic and Eastern Orthodox Churches in 1054. But the arguments only make sense if you affirm a Trinitarian theology in the first place. Muslims and Jews find the entire argument moot since they cannot imagine a God who is one–in–three or three–in–one. Hindus would find the argument unnecessary since they believe all things, physical as well as spiritual, are manifestations of the one God, Brahman. And Buddhists would consider this a great waste of energy since they don't posit a Creator God in the first place.

So when someone asks you whether or not you believe in God, make sure to have the questioner clarify what she or he means by *God*. Without such clarification the question is meaningless and unanswerable.

I start with this because this book is a guide to God, and you need to know what definition of *God* I am using if you are to decide whether or not reading this book is going to guide you somewhere you wish to go. Lucky for you, this is the *Rabbi Rami Guide to God* so you don't have to wade through centuries of theological argument within and among the world's religions to find out what the word *God* means in this context. All you have to do is ask Rabbi Rami what he means when he uses the word *God*.

Lucky for me, I am Rabbi Rami so I don't have to bother with all that theological speculation either. I can simply tell you that by *God* I mean the Source and Substance of all reality. God is all there ever was, is, and will be; God is both infinite potential and finite actualizations of that potential. To be as clear as I can be, for me God is all that is, and all that is may surpass all we know there to be.

My *God* is the God of the Perennial Philosophy, a recurring wisdom that crops up among the mystics of every age and in every culture. Hence, the *Rabbi Rami Guide to God* isn't a guide to the Jewish God, the Christian God, the Muslim God, the Hindu God, or any other deity of any other of the hundreds of religions we humans have imagined over the millennia. It is Rabbi Rami's guide to Rabbi Rami's God, who I just happen to think is the one true God.

It is important to remember this. If you are looking for insight into the Gods of one religion or another, or if you are fearful of entertaining any idea of God other than your own, let me save you some time, money, and effort: this book is not for you. Don't read it. It will only upset you, and life is upsetting enough without me bothering you. So, no hard feelings; just finish this sentence, close the book, and walk away. Bye.

If you're still reading you have no one to blame but yourself. I warned you: this is a guide to the God of the Perennial Philosophy, and while it will draw on the teachings of Perennial Philosophers from many religions, it is unconcerned with the official theologies of those religions.

Reading this guide will not make you a better Hindu, Jew, Christian, Muslim, Baha'i, Sikh, Pagan, or Wiccan. In fact it won't even make you a better person. Reading rarely does that. But if you engage in some of the spiritual practices mentioned in this guide, you might make yourself a better person.

So let me be clear: I am a Perennialist. I believe that human beings are capable of directly experiencing God because I believe we are always and already an expression or extension of God. I don't believe one religion is right and others are wrong. I believe that any religion when seen through the lens of the Perennial Philosophy, which most often means through the eyes of its mystics rather than its clerics, can lead you to God and your innate oneness with God, when God is understood as the Source and Substance of all reality.

The *Rabbi Rami Guide to God*, like all the other books in the Rabbi Rami Guide series, is a blend of theory and practice. I provide the theory, but you must do the practices. No one can experience God for you. You have to do this yourself. Like any guidebook, this one only points toward something. If you want to get to know Paris, for example, it is wise to bring a guidebook, but it is essential to wander the streets for yourself. The same is true here: if you want to know about God, read this guide. If you want to know God directly, practice.

What is the
Perennial Philosophy?

THE TERM *perennial philosophy* was coined in 1540 by Agostino Steuco. Steuco argued that many of the pre–Christian teachings of ancient Greece and Rome supported Catholic teaching as well. A loyal son of the Church, Steuco wasn't interested in articulating a truth outside Catholicism, only in showing that Catholicism was not at odds with earlier wisdom, but a more mature and divinely revealed flowering of it. Today's global understanding of the Perennial Philosophy was articulated by German mathematician and philosopher Gottfried Leibnitz (1646–1716). Leibnitz argued that there is a universal and eternal philosophy underlying all religions (not just Steuco's Catholicism) that is reflected most clearly in the mystical teachings of every religion.

Not every religion lays claim to a mystical tradition, and even those that do are often disinclined to focus on it. But for our purposes, suffice it to say that mystics are those who engage in contemplative practices designed to bring them into direct contact with Reality—what I am calling God. A mystic is not all that concerned with theology, preferring to eat the meal rather than argue over the menu. And when they do, when they "taste and see" the reality of God (Psalm 34:8), they discover that what they are tasting is what all mystics are tasting, even if they call it by different names.

> *Truth is one. Different people call it by different names.*
> RIG VEDA

14

Giving Steuco and Liebnitz their due, it was Aldous Huxley who made the Perennial Philosophy part of the contemporary spiritual conversation with the publication of his book *The Perennial Philosophy* in 1945. The book was a collection of texts and teachings from the world's religions that suggested a shared wisdom that each of them possessed. Two years later, in an introduction to Christopher Isherwood and Swami Prabhavananda's translation of the Hindu spiritual classic Bhagavad Gita, "the Song of God," Huxley articulated four universal points of agreement among mystics of every faith:

FIRST: The phenomenal world of matter and of individualized consciousness—the world of things and animals and men and even gods— is the manifestation of a Divine Ground within which all partial realities have their being, and apart from which they would be non–existent.

SECOND: Human beings are capable not merely of knowing about the Divine Ground by infer- ence; they can also realize its existence by a direct intuition, superior to discursive reasoning. This immediate knowledge unites the knower with that which is known.

THIRD: Man possesses a double nature, a phenom- enal ego and an eternal Self, which is the inner man, the spirit, the spark of divinity within the soul. It is possible for a man, if he so desires, to identify himself with the spirit and therefore with the Divine Ground, which is of the same or like nature with the spirit.

15

FOURTH: Man's life on earth has only one end and purpose: to identify himself with his eternal Self and so to come to unitive knowledge of the Divine Ground. (Bhagavad-Gita, NY: Signet Classics, 2002)

Just so we are perfectly clear, let me simplify Huxley's language a bit. The Perennial Philosophy asserts 1) everything is a manifestation of God; 2) people have an innate capacity to directly intuit God, and when they do they realize the unity of all things in, with, and as God; 3) human beings can see themselves as both apart from and a part of God, and can, if they choose, overcome the alienation and ignorance that comes with the former by engaging in practices that make clear the latter; and 4) the sole purpose of human life is to realize God as the singular Reality manifesting as nature's wondrous diversity.

This is a very big claim. And unlike theological positions that one is challenged to accept on faith alone, this claim can be tested. It doesn't matter that sages of every faith throughout time and across all cultures have said something to this effect. What matters is that they also offered you a means to test their experience

16

by making it your own. You can prove or disprove the validity of the Perennial Philosophy by engaging in the spiritual practices of the Perennial Philosophers and seeing for yourself what is so.

Believe nothing on faith alone, no matter how ancient and revered. Believe nothing simply because it is popular, or because old sages taught it. Believe nothing of your imagining and do not be deluded into thinking yourself a prophet. Believe nothing on the say so of the powerful. Believe only what you yourself have tested and found reasonable. And then live according to that.

BUDDHA

But why test this? Why bother with the Perennial Philosophy when there are so many others to choose from? I would offer two answers. First, when I look to the lives of those saints and sages who espouse this philosophy, I often see women and men of great compassion whose lives I want to imitate. Second, the promise of the Perennial Philosophy holds out a cure for the primary dis-ease that haunts me: the notion that I am apart from rather than a part of God.

17

Chances are one or both of these reasons speak to you as well. First, you know your life could be more loving, just, and compassionate; and you see in the great mystics of the world the qualities of love, justice, and compassion that you wish to cultivate. If you want what they have, you must practice as they practiced. Second, you may also have that nagging sense of isolation systemic to the ego that imagines a world of endless competition and consumption, and which drives you to distraction and desperation in search of something that will bring you fulfillment and peace. If you do and if you are, the Perennial Philosophy says, "Stop chasing after the wind. What you want is what you already have, who you already are. Learn how to be who you really are, and alienation, fear, anxiety, and ignorance dissolve, and you are free to love and be loved without concern for dogma, doctrine, and religious labels."

Not everyone likes the Perennial Philosophy. Some dislike it because it undermines the notion that one religion is true and the others false. Others dislike it because it seems so static while human beings and life in general are dynamic.

To the former I say, "Relax. Don't worry about

18

it. There is no need to be a Perennialist; it's just another label. Stick with the religion you prefer, just go beneath the surface. Every religion has its exoteric dimension, the level of doctrine and rules, the side that focuses on who wins and who loses; just don't imagine that the exoteric is all your religion has to offer. Look deeper and you will find the wisdom of the esoteric dimension, the wisdom lived by the greatest saints.

Frithjof Schuon, a leading scholar of the Perennial Philosophy, or what he preferred to call the Primordial Philosophy, urges us to imagine the world's religions as so many mountain islands dotting the sea. From the surface of the water each appears separate, unique, and complete unto itself. But if you dive beneath the surface of the sea you will discover that each mountain is an outcropping of a singular land formation. Each mountain is still unique, but no longer separate from all the others or the greater ground from which they all arise.

19

The point is there is no need to go outside your religion; just don't be satisfied with the surface of your religion. Dive deeper. Every religion has spiritual practices that will bring you to God–realization. Call it the Perennial Philosophy or call it something else, the experience is the same, and the result is a life overflowing with love.

> *By love I do not mean any natural tenderness, which is more or less in people according to their constitution; but I mean a larger principle of the soul, founded in reason and piety, which makes us tender, kind, and gentle to all our fellow creatures as creatures of God, and for God's sake.*
>
> WILLIAM LAW

To those who worry that the Perennial Philosophy is too static, that it can't speak to the challenges of our time, I admit that even the greatest mystics are bound by the social mores of their age. When I read these great sages I don't seek to imitate their life styles. Neither the Buddha nor the Baal Shem Tov liberated women from their respective cultural shackles, for example. What I look for is confirmation that through spiritual practice we human beings can overcome our sense of alienation from one another, from nature, and from God. I then seek to do so, trusting that I will live from that unity in a way appropriate to my time rather than their time.

When the author of Leviticus tapped into the Divine Reality and wrote, "You shall love your neighbor as yourself," (Leviticus 19:18), he most likely understood his "neighbor" to be his fellow Israelites. When Jesus tapped into the same Reality and heralded the same commandment (Matthew 22:39), he most likely understood his "neighbor" to include all human beings. Today when I read that command, I understand "neighbor" to include my fellow Jews, my fellow human beings, and all other species of life on this or any other planet. The Priestly writer of Leviticus, Jesus, and I are all tapping into the same Wisdom, but we are able to apply it in ever more expansive ways. It isn't that Jesus found something better than love, it is just that he could love more inclusively. It isn't that you and I will find something better than love, only that living some twenty centuries after Jesus we can use that love to embrace an ever widening circle of living beings. The Perennial Philosophy is dynamic because people are dynamic. Wisdom is one; people learn to live it in ever more expansive ways.

21

> *If religion is to bring light to our broken world, we need, as Mencius suggested, to go in search of the lost heart, the spirit of compassion that lies at the core of all our traditions.*
>
> KAREN ARMSTRONG

I became a Perennialist in theory when I read Huston Smith's *The Religions of Man* in high school. (Dr. Smith's book is still a widely used introduction to religion, though like the Perennial Philosophy it espouses, the book can adapt to the times and is today called *The World's Religions*.) Although I began my meditation practice during this time, it did not mature until decades later. When it did, I discovered not only the unity of all things in the One which I call God, but that this realization began a transformation of my personality. It was not enough to just know God; knowing God leads one to doing—to doing good.

By engaging in the practices you will find in this Guide, you will be walking a path toward *metanoia*, a Greek word meaning a fundamental transformation of your heart and mind.

> *I feel, my dear Lucilius, that I am being not only reformed but transformed.*
>
> SENECA

From the Perennialist perspective, this transformation is the true value of spiritual practice. Our aim is not simply to know about God, but to experience God as all reality, and in so doing to transform our lives with love.

The remainder of this Guide explores each of the four points of the Perennial Philosophy, one in each chapter, addressing how each speaks to some of the challenges of life. Chapter Five will introduce a contemporary expression of the Perennial Philosophy articulated by Father Thomas Keating and the Snowmass Group, a gathering of contemplatives with whom I have been associated since the group's founding in 1984. Chapter Six will offer a simple and universal spiritual practice to help you move from being informed by this Guide to being transformed by the God toward which it points.

As with all of the Rabbi Rami Guides, I am indebted to the wisdom and editorial skills of Victoria

23

Sutherland, and the trust and entrepreneurial passion of the people at *Spirituality & Health* magazine who publish this series. To them and to you I offer my thanks. And to you all, I remind you that these guides are fingers pointing to the moon, and never the moon itself. Don't get distracted.

CHAPTER ONE

All Is God

> *The phenomenal world of matter and of individualized*
> *consciousness—the world of things and animals*
> *and men and even gods—is the manifestation of a*
> *Divine Ground within which all partial realities have*
> *their being, and apart from which they would be*
> *non–existent.*
>
> ALDOUS HUXLEY

IMAGINE YOU ARE SITTING in front of a huge pie pan
filled with Play-Doh. If imagining is too hard, or if
you want to explore the Perennial Philosophy with
your kids, go get some Play-Doh and fill a pan with
it. When you have the Play-Doh in front of you, imagined or otherwise, begin to pull the modeling clay into
a variety of shapes without removing any of the Play-

Doh from the pan. Pull up people, animals, houses, mountains, trees, etc. Don't worry about your skills as a sculptor, just end up with a world of beings and structures all arising from a single pan of Play-Doh.

This is what Huxley means by his notion that the phenomenal world, the world inside our heads and outside our heads, the world of thoughts, feelings, and stuff all arises from and in the same Divine Ground—God.

> *In the beginning there was Existence alone—One only without a second. It, the One, thought to Itself: "Let Me be many, let Me grow forth." Thus, out of Itself, It projected the universe and having projected the universe out of Itself, It entered into every being, All that is has its self in It alone. Of all things It is the subtle essence. It is the truth. It is the self. And you are That.*
>
> CHANDOGYA UPANISHAD

This is often difficult for people to grasp: "I'm God? I don't feel like God. I don't control the universe like God. How can I be God?" The difficulty arises from the definition most people have of the word *God*. If you define God as an all-powerful, all-knowing Being outside the created world of time and space who created the world and governs its inhabitants, holding out reward from those who do your will and punishment for those who thwart it, then saying "I am God" seems and is silly. Even delusional. But if you define God the way I do, as the Source and Substance of all reality, then to insist you are other than God is delusional. As I said earlier, it all depends on how you think about God.

There are five general ways people think about God: theist, atheist, agnostic, pantheist, and panentheist.

THEISTS

Theists believe that God exists, is self-aware, lives somewhere outside time and space, is the creator or catalyst for creation, sets a standard for human behavior, judges us against that standard, and rewards and punishes us accordingly either in this life, some future life, or in a supernatural spirit world like heaven or hell.

Some theists, called monotheists, believe there is only one God, while others, called polytheists believer there are many Gods. Our concern here is with monotheists who believe there is a supernatural, self-aware creator who guides and judges the world, rewarding and punishing us humans in this life or some other.

ATHEISTS

While it might seem odd, those thinkers about God closest to monotheists are in fact atheists. The "a" prefacing "theist" means "not." Atheists are not theists, or, more accurately, atheists deny what theists believe. Atheists do not propose a theology of their own, but rather deny the reality of all theology by denying the reality of God. This sounds simple enough, but it isn't. In fact, atheists only deny one way of looking at God, the theistic way.

Atheists and theists agree on the basic meaning of the word *God*. For both atheists and theists, God is a supernatural, self-aware creator who guides and judges the world, rewarding and punishing us humans in this life or some other. The difference between the two isn't their definition of the word *God* but their sense as to whether the word refers to anything beyond itself.

Imagine you and I are having a discussion about

unicorns. We both agree that a unicorn is a large white winged horse with a single spiral horn extending from the middle of its forehead. No argument here. When either one of us speaks of unicorns we know exactly what the other means, and use the word in the same way. Where we might disagree is over the notion that unicorns exist or used to exist as living beings the way horses do today. You may say unicorns do exist, I would argue they do not. For you *unicorn* may refer to a species of animal living or extinct, where I would say they are imaginary creatures who only exist in legend and fairy tale.

Our positions are irreconcilable, even though we both agree as to the meaning of the word. This is the situation in which monotheists and atheists find themselves. They agree as to what *God* means, and disagree as to whether God is or was. The theists say God exists outside the world of words, and atheists say God only exists within the stories we tell and not in the "real" world we live in daily.

AGNOSTICS

Agnostics often claim to fall in between theists and atheists. Along with theists and atheists, agnostics understand the word *God* to mean a supernatural, self-aware creator who guides and judges the world, rewarding and punishing us humans in this life or some other. Where the theist affirms the existence of such a being, and the atheist denies its existence, the agnostic claims to keep an open mind. Like the "a" in "atheist," the "a" in "agnostic" represents a negative, a denial. But what the agnostic denies isn't *theos*, God, but *gnosis*, knowledge. The agnostic says there is insufficient evidence to prove or disprove the existence of God, and so seeks to keep an open mind.

On the surface the agnostic position may seem the wiser of the three. Even the theist will admit that the existence of God cannot be proven, especially if by proof you mean scientific, verifiable proof that can be demonstrated in a laboratory under strict scientific conditions. That is why the theist will often take refuge in faith: "I believe in God," the theist might say, "even though I cannot know with scientific certainty." Faith is a matter of conviction or feeling, not scientific proof.

The problem with the agnostics isn't their position in the debate, but in their behavior. Ask most agnostics what church, mosque, synagogue, or temple they attend, and most will look at you as if you just landed from Mars. Most agnostics don't join religions or adhere to any specific religious doctrine or practice. How can they? Without any knowledge (*gnosis*) of God, how would they know which God to worship and which religion to join? So when it comes to behavior, the agnostic is indistinguishable from the atheist. Not knowing for certain if God exists seems to lead to behavior that matches those who are certain that God does not exist.

The agnostic position led the French philosopher Blaise Pascal to pose what is today called Pascal's Wager. It goes something like this: While it is true that you cannot know whether or not God exists, it is also true that you have to make certain choices regarding how you will live. If you choose to live without God and religion, and it turns out that God does exist, the punishment for your unbelief could be severe. If, on the other hand, you choose to live as if God exists and it turns out God does not exist, nothing is gained but nothing is lost. So, Pascal says, it is better to live as a theist even if one is agnostic.

Perhaps this makes sense to you. It certainly did to Pascal. But Pascal had one great advantage over us:

his choice of God and religion was limited to one, the Catholic Church. Today you would have a plethora of Gods and religions from which to choose. Should you be a Catholic or a Lutheran or a Wiccan? Should you follow the way of the Southern Baptist or the Sunni Muslim or the Theravadan Buddhist? Perhaps Judaism is true, or perhaps it is the Sikh, Mormon, or Hindu religions that hold the key to salvation. You can't know for sure. So which will you choose? You can still believe that Pascal is right: it is better to live as a theist even if you are an agnostic, but which theism shall you follow? Choose wrongly and, if the God of some other religion turns out to be the true God, your fate is as dismal as if you simply avoided God and joined the atheist camp.

You could, of course, simply affirm the existence of God and assume that being a good person is all God requires, but this is no less a guess than any other choice. An agnostic must learn to live with the ambiguity and potential damnation of refusing to choose.

PANTHEIST

While monotheists, atheists, and agnostics are variations on a theme, each accepting the same definition of the word *God*, and differing only over whether such a being actually exists, with the pantheist the definition changes completely.

Where our first three thinkers posit a God separate from nature, the pantheist sees God as synonymous with nature. God is what is; nothing other or apart, God is the very stuff of reality itself. God may or may not be self-conscious depending on whether or not you believe plants and rocks are self-conscious. Or the pantheist may argue that God is self-conscious to the extent that there are self-conscious beings in nature. Humans, to name but one species, are self-conscious; since humans are part of God, then God is to that extent self-conscious as well. Indeed, humans may be the way God achieves self-consciousness in this place at this time.

While pantheists come in as many variations as theists, they all see an equivalence between nature and God. This is what pantheist means: *pan*/all is, *theos*/God. The advantage pantheists have over theists is that by equating God and nature, the pantheist has no need to posit a supernatural realm that cannot be proven. If you ask a pantheist whether or not God exists, she will answer unequivocally: "Yes, God exists.

God is nature. Nature exists and can be proven to exist, so God exists."

> *Everyone is included in God. The world is identical with God.*
>
> THE KORETZER REBBE

Given this definition, it may be that many who call themselves atheists and agnostics would feel quite at home in pantheism. What do pantheists worship? Many do not worship at all, not in the sense of supplicating oneself to a supernatural God, but many do work to cultivate a sense of gratitude toward life, and feel a deep sense of awe and responsibility with regard to the natural world. Where a theist might pray to God for rain, a pantheist would seek to understand the laws of nature that cause rain to happen. And both would be grateful for the rain when it comes.

PANENTHEISM

The first cousin of the pantheist is the panentheist. The difference between them is in the little word *en*/in. Where the pantheist believes all is God, the panentheist believes all is in God, but God is still greater than the sum of nature's parts. Like the pantheist, the panentheist sees no division between God and nature, but unlike the pantheist, the panentheist imagines God as greater than, albeit, not separate from nature.

> *The Being of God includes and penetrates the whole universe, so that every part exists in Him, but His Being is more than, and not exhausted by, the universe.*
>
> THE OXFORD DICTIONARY
> OF THE CHRISTIAN CHURCH

Think in terms of an ocean and its waves. The waves are not other than the ocean, but the ocean is more than its waves. This is the panentheist position. You and I and all reality is not other than God, but God is still greater than us. And because God is greater than what was and is at the moment, what will be can be surprisingly different as well. The panentheist puts creative surprise at the heart of God.

Perennial Philosophers tend to fall into the pantheist or panentheist camps. In the interest of full

35

disclosure, I am a panentheist. I believe God is all of me, though I am not all of God.

> *God is that "in whom we live and move and have our being."*
>
> ST. PAUL, QUOTED IN THE BOOK OF ACTS 17:28

Back to our pan of Play-Doh. Everything that exists in the world of Play-Doh is made of Play-Doh. Yet everything that exists is not everything that can exist. You are free to flatten a few things and make new ones. And, imagining both pan and Play-Doh to be infinite and timeless, "There are more things in heaven and earth, Horatio, than are dreamt of in your pan of Play-Doh," (my apologies to Shakespeare).

Of course my little Play-Doh analogy isn't perfect. You still need an outside force to form the beings who inhabit the Play-Doh universe. You could, if you insist, take the same analogy and use it to prove two points: 1) the interdependence of all created life (we are all made of Play-Doh), and 2) the need of an outside Creator. Without that external God, a pan of flat Play-Doh will never be anything other than a pan of flat Play-Doh.

The panentheist, and most Perennialists are panentheists, would respond to this challenge by affirming that God, Reality, is intrinsically creative, and hence the Play-Doh would form and transform itself over and over and over simply for the sheer joy of creating. Both panentheists and theists affirm the creativity of God. They differ only in that the theist insists God and creativity are not part of the world, which in and of itself is pretty dumb and in need of outside divine intervention to do anything, while the panentheist insists the universe, being a manifestation of God, is itself intrinsically creative because God is intrinsically creative.

Does the difference matter? It depends upon whom you ask. Does it matter to you? I can't say. Does it matters to me? Absolutely. It matters to me because the panentheist position sees the world as holy, as creative, and surprising. And it sees you and me as no less so. It matters to me because the panentheist position reveals my unity with nature, and affirms nature's capacity for self-consciousness. And it matters to me because it reveals that all life is my neighbor, and all my neighbors are my self.

We recall Leviticus 18:19, "You shall love your

37

RABBI RAMI **GUIDE TO GOD**

neighbor as yourself." It doesn't say "You shall love your neighbor as you love yourself." The key isn't love but the realization that you and your neighbor are a single self. I mentioned earlier that the text originally referred to Israelites alone. Jesus read it more broadly: your neighbor is any and every human being. I read it more broadly still, all living things are your neighbor, and there is nothing that isn't living. You shall love all things as your self. In other words, when you come to realize that there is only one self, God, and this self includes you and all life, love for all things arises of its own accord.

This is why perennialism matters and why, for me, panentheism is true: it leads to love.

"
*Love is from the infinite, and will remain until
     eternity.*
*The seeker of love escapes the chains of birth
     and death.*
Tomorrow, when resurrection comes,
The heart that is not in love will fail the test.

RUMI, "THIEF OF SLEEP,"
TRANSLATED BY SHAHRAM SHIVA
"

CHAPTER TWO

A Direct Knowing of God

> *Human beings are capable not merely of knowing about the Divine Ground by inference; they can also realize its existence by a direct intuition, superior to discursive reasoning. This immediate knowledge unites the knower with that which is known.*
>
> ALDOUS HUXLEY

PROOFS OF GOD'S EXISTENCE fall into two categories: objective and subjective. Objective proofs start with the assumption that reason can make the existence of God axiomatic. Subjective proofs begin with the notion that experience is the same as truth.

Here are three of the more well-known objective proofs of God's existence:

1. Cosmological Argument: Everything has a cause. The universe must have a cause. God is the cause of the universe. Therefore, God exists.

2. Ontological Argument: God is perfect. Nonexistence is imperfect. Therefore, God exists.

3. Teleological Argument: The world is sublimely ordered. Nothing so ordered can order itself; it must have a cause. See Argument 1.

These arguments still speak to lots of people today, but they do not speak to me. Saying that everything has a cause implies that God, too, has a cause. Simply saying that everything has a cause but God, who has no cause, is an assertion of a truth rather than proof of one. Defining God as perfect already presupposes the existence of the very thing we want to prove. And why claim that existence is more perfect that nonexistence? It seems to me that existence and nonexistence go with one another the way up goes with down and in goes with out. I cannot understand any one of these terms without its opposite. Perfection to me would include both existence and nonexistence. So we cannot limit God to either state. And while I admit to and admire the order of the cosmos, I can explain it through billions and billions of years of natural selection. Or, if I can't, I am once again left with the notion that everything has a cause except God, an argument that is arbitrary rather than logical.

Those, like me, who find these logical proofs of God's existence less than compelling often turn to subjective experience to prove that God is real. This might be called the Phenomenological Argument for God: People experience God as a real phenomenon. Therefore, God exists.

What I like about the Phenomenological Argument is that it is based on lived experience. This is also what I hate about it. Have you ever experienced a mirage and seen water that just wasn't there? Have you ever noticed that when you place a pencil in a glass of water it appears bent when viewed from the side of the glass? Have you ever mistaken a rope for a snake? People have all kinds of perceptions that have no basis in reality.

41

My sister, Debbie, for example, believes beyond a shadow of a doubt that our family had a dog named Bowser, despite the fact that there are no photographs of the dog, and neither my parents nor I have any memories of him. I cannot prove that Bowser didn't exist, and she cannot prove that he did. But she has the weight of memory on her side. She knew the dog none of us can remember. Does this prove that Bowser was real? I don't think so. Just having an experience proves nothing other than people can have experiences.

I know several very intelligent and thoughtful people who have had personal and palpable encounters with God. One, a deeply passionate Protestant layperson, swears he felt the presence of Jesus Christ in his daughter's hospital room as she breathed her last breath. Another, a Tibetan Buddhist lama, has told me that he has stood in the presence of several Tibetan deities as a result of months of meditative training. I do not doubt their sincerity, nor do I doubt that both experienced something profoundly meaningful to each of them. But I cannot extrapolate from either report that God exists, or that, if God does exist, God is Christian or Tibetan.

In other words, personal experience of God is not

proof of God's existence, only proof that people can have experiences they associate with God. And yet the second of Huxley's four points of the Perennial Philosophy states that God can be directly known, and that the knowing somehow reveals the unity of knower with the Known. Is this true?

I can attest from personal experience that it is true that one can have experiences during meditative practice in which one perceives a greater reality of which all things are a part. But am I willing to say that my experience of this greater reality that I call God proves the existence of God? No. All I can prove is that experiences similar to mine are not rare, that they occur among peoples of every culture and religion, and have done so across the centuries. But just because people everywhere can mistake a rope for a snake doesn't mean that snakes are really ropes in disguise.

I am doing my best to undermine the proof offered by my own religious position, that of the Perennial Philosophy. I am doing so because the benefit of the experience isn't in proving the existence of God, however defined, but in the psycho-spiritual transformation such experiences entail.

Let me make this as clear as I can. If you ask me if I

43

believe in God, I will say "yes, if by God you mean the Source and Substance of all reality." If you accept my definition and ask me why I believe, I will say that I not only believe, but I know that God exists because I have had many experiences of God manifesting in me, through me, and as me, and in, through, and as everything else; and that these experiences are so real to me that I cannot speak differently about God. If you then ask me if my experiences are sufficient to prove the existence of God, I would say "no." They are simply my experiences, and may have no validity outside my own mind. My certainty of God is no more reliable than my sister's certainty of Bowser.

It is often at this point in a conversation about God that people raise the Bible as proof not only of God's existence but the truth claims of Judaism (if they are Jews) or Christianity (if they are Christians). The Bible is, they will tell me, the Word of God. How can there be a Word if there is no God? The problem with this argument is that it can be applied to any sacred text. Are Jews and Christians willing to extend their argument to the Bhagavad Gita of the Hindus, and affirm that Krishna is God?

Sacred texts of any tradition will inevitably affirm

44

the truths of that tradition. The Jewish Bible tells us the Jews are God's Chosen. What else would it say? The Christian Bible affirms that Jesus is the Christ. Could it say anything different? Could the Book of Mormon do anything but support the claims of the Mormon faith? So if you are going to choose one sacred text among many to prove one religious claim among many, simply know that doing so proves nothing. This is often quite shocking to people.

When my Christian students, for example, seek to prove to me that Jesus is Christ they point to the New Testament as proof. When I tell them that Jews do not accept the New Testament as the Word of God they are shocked. It never occurred to them that it could be anything else. Why, they ask me, do you believe that God's revelation would stop with the Hebrew Bible? My answer is simple, "For the same reason you believe it stops with the New Testament and not with the Qur'an; and for the same reason Muslims believe it stops with the Qur'an and not with the revelations of Bahaullah, the prophet of the Baha'i faith. We choose to call those texts sacred which affirm our beliefs, while rejecting as secular those that do not. The reasoning is self-serving and circular, and not at all compelling."

45

There are no proofs of God that are universally compelling. And certainly no proof for any particular God—Jewish, Christian, Muslim, Hindu, etc.—that speaks to people outside the faith system devoted to that particular God. There are only people seeking to prove their understanding of God either objectively or subjectively. I am not moved by either, and find both such efforts irrelevant.

Enter C. S. Lewis. I add this here only because so many Christians tend to bring him into the conversation at this point, and while I am not dealing with Christianity per se, what he says is applicable to all religions. In his book *Mere Christianity,* Mr. Lewis argues that Jesus is either the Lord, a liar, or a lunatic. Since few would call him liar or lunatic, he must be Lord. But this is a false choice.

Why are we limited to just these three options? When Jesus says, for example, "I and the Father are one," (John 10:30), I understand him from the perspective of the Perennial Philosophy and celebrate his discovery. He is one with God, and so are you. When Jesus says, "I am the way and the truth and the life. No one comes to the Father except through me," (John 14:6), I don't see him as a megalomaniac but as a mystic. Jesus

46

is saying that to realize your unity with God you must achieve that level of consciousness he has achieved, what St. Paul calls the Mind of Christ and that mystics of all religions speak of in their own way.

In other words, from the Perennialist point of view, you need not defend your religion or attack another's. You need only broaden your understanding of religion to include the mystical perspective of God in, with, and as all reality, and then read your scripture from that wisdom.

The Perennial Philosophy's notion that you can directly experience the Divine Ground, God as the Source and Substance of all reality, has nothing to do with proof. The goal is not to prove God, but to be changed by God. It is the experience of transcending your sense of separateness, of discovering yourself to be part of the whole of reality—whether you call this greater reality God or something else—that matters. What matters is what happens to you when you have this experience. And the first thing that happens is the uniting of knower and known.

All existent entities exist by the power of God's reality. God's knowledge of the world is totally different from

human knowledge. He knows himself, and knowing himself, he knows the whole universe, and nothing escapes him. He knows his reality as it is, not by knowledge external to himself the way we know. For we and our knowledge are not one, whereas the Creator and his knowledge and life are one in every respect. He is the knower, he is the known, and he is the knowledge itself, all of it being one.

MAIMONIDES

Toss an ice cube in a bowl of warm water. Over time the ice will melt, and it will simply merge with the water in the bowl. The ice cube loses its form, but not its essence. Its essence is H_2O, not other than that of the water in the bowl. Its shape as a cube allowed it to stand out from the rest of the water in the bowl for a time, but eventually it will be no more, but it won't be less.

This is what happens to you during meditation or some other contemplative practice. You begin as a seemingly separate form, and in time that form dissolves and you discover for a moment that you aren't the form, but that which comprises it, and that which comprises it is the same reality that comprises everything else. You are the knower seeking to know the Divine Ground, as Huxley called it. At first the Divine seems other than you, but in the end you discover there is no other, there is only the Divine manifesting—like our Play-Doh metaphor has already reminded us—as everything. When the knower (you) knows itself to be the known (God), the knower is no longer other than the known, both disappear in the experience of knowing. Which is when the whole thing becomes very confusing.

If you disappear, who knows you have disappeared? If you melt into the water of the bowl, who is there to remember you were once the cube? Language fails us here. There are no words for the experience I am hinting at, and that is because there is no real experience because there is no one to experience it.

I know this sounds crazy. That is why mystics talk less and practice more. I cannot explain the taste of chocolate to you, but I can offer you a piece that you can taste for yourself. That is what I am doing in this Guide. Right now I am *talking* about chocolate, later I will offer you a piece. Hopefully my talking about it will make you curious and courageous enough to "taste and see."

But let's not make this too easy. If there is no "me" to know there is no "me," why do I say there's no "me"? It isn't that I am experiencing the unity of all things in, with, and as God. If that were true, then the unity of all things in, with, and as God would not include me, and therefore would not be a true unity. The only way I know a thing is by differentiating myself from it. But there is no differentiation in this unity, so there is no knowing, no experiencing. And, indeed, this is my "experience."

When these moments of unity arise, I know them only by hindsight. I assume unity "happened" based on the experience I have after the unity moment has passed and my sense of separate self returns. Reb Nachman of Bratslav, one of the great Jewish mystics of the nineteenth century, has a word for this; he calls it *reshimu*. Imagine you purchase a bottle of fine perfume, remove the stopper, and allow the perfume to evaporate into the air. When the bottle is empty it still retains the fragrance of the perfume even though the oil itself is gone. From the fragrance I can assume that the bottle once contained perfume. *Reshimu* is the residual impression of the perfume.

When I dissolve in meditation—something that doesn't happen regularly, but that has happened often enough for me to take it seriously—I return to find the fragrance of the experience lingering within and around me. I don't know what it is like to be gone, but I do know what it is like to return. My sense of self is lighter, more malleable, less fixed and rigid. I feel a genuine love for and from everything around me. I feel the trees (I often do my spiritual practice outdoors along a river bank), the birds, the deer, the squirrels, as extensions of myself, and myself as somehow an extension of them. If there are other people in the vicinity, they too seem to be part of a "me" that embraces and transcends the body of which I am becoming more aware. If the emptying into God was—what, long enough? deep enough? (such qualities really do not apply); I find that the rocks and stones and even the garbage I notice is all part of the Divine Ground.

For me the feeling fades all too quickly, but for others it can last a lifetime. Yet even for me, it is an experience worth having, cherishing, pursuing day after day. Do I meditate in order to experience the divine *reshimu*? I used to. When I was young, when this experience was so new and so wondrous, I craved it the way others might crave a good steak. But, thankfully, I no longer meditate for any other reason than I enjoy sitting in silence, or walking and chanting in the forest by my home.

There is no guarantee that meditation will lead to realization, and there are other ways to slip the bonds of the separate self and melt into the greater reality of God—running, swimming, knitting, and all manner of sports that require concentration—so I am not saying you should or can meditate your way to enlightenment. You can't.

A Zen master once inquired of a monk meditating on a large boulder, "What are you doing?" The monk replied, "I am meditating so as to achieve enlightenment." The master sat down next to the monk and began to noisily polish a rock with his robe. Annoyed, the monk said, "Master, what are you doing?" "I am polishing this stone to make a mirror." "But master, the monk said, "no matter how long you polish that stone it will never become a mirror." "Just so with your meditation," the master said, "no matter how long you sit here you will never become enlightened."

ZEN PARABLE

But it doesn't matter. What matters is that through regular contemplative practice you change in the one way that matters most: you become more compassionate.

Great compassion penetrates into the marrow of the bone.

NARGARJUNA

53

CHAPTER THREE

Our Dual Nature

> *Man possesses a double nature, a phenomenal ego and an eternal Self, which is the inner man, the spirit, the spark of divinity within the soul. It is possible for a man, if he so desires, to identify himself with the spirit and therefore with the Divine Ground, which is of the same or like nature with the spirit.*
>
> ALDOUS HUXLEY

YOU ARE NOT WHO YOU THINK YOU ARE.

Stand in front of a mirror and look at yourself. Who is looking? It isn't your body, because the you who is looking is aware of the body and must therefore be other than the body. It isn't your emotions, those judgments that arise from observing your body: you're too thin, you're too fat, you're too this, you're too that, because you are aware of those feelings and the you who is aware isn't feeling those things. It isn't your thoughts for the same reason: you are aware of your thoughts and the you who is thus aware isn't one of those thoughts. So is there a *you* separate from body, heart, and mind? It certainly seems this way.

Who is this *you*? Don't simply say, "It is me," since you must then answer the question who is the *you* that is saying "It is me"? Every time you look to see who you are, you discover a *you* behind that you; a you that cannot be seen. This you cannot be seen and only sees; this you cannot be known and only knows; this you has no name, no gender, no age, no location, no qualities of any kind. It is simply awareness.

This is what Huxley calls the eternal Self, or what Hindus might call *Atman*, or what Jews, Christians, and Muslims might call Soul. But let us not be too quick to assume these are all different words for the same thing. When I speak to practitioners of various religions that posit a soul or atman, there is the tendency to identify egoically with that greater Self. People speak of "my soul" and even "my atman." But this is not what the Perennial Philosophy is talking about.

Huxley's eternal Self is the atman only if you understand the meaning of the Hindu teaching, "Atman is Brahman," Atman is God. Huxley's eternal Self is the soul only if you believe that there is but one soul, God, animating all life. There is only one eternal Self: the nameless, formless, attribute–free awareness that is aware of you at this very moment.

Ask yourself: "Who is reading this book right now?" Immediately you will become aware of yourself sitting on a couch or a chair reading, but who is it that is aware of this? As you become aware of this other knower, you will realize that you are not that either, but yet a more subtle knowing that has no name and is not yet an object.

You might think this is just a game; a projection of a nameless knower/knowing *ad nauseum*. Perhaps it is. I am willing to doubt everything I think I know about God and self. I am only interested in what this knowing does to me, how it makes me kinder and more compassionate. But I suspect there is more to it than a game.

Rather than think in terms of infinite regression or progression, think in terms of paradox. Your eyes can see everything but themselves; your teeth can bite everything but themselves; your tongue can lick anything but itself. In this way, you can encounter everything but your own Self. This is because the Self cannot be made into an object. It is the eternal Subject. And while it is you, it isn't yours.

> So tell me: Who are you? You are not your thoughts, for you are aware of them. You are not your feelings, for you are aware of them. You are not any objects that you can see for you are aware of them too. Something in you is aware of all these things. So tell me: What is it in you that is conscious of everything? . . . That vast witnessing awareness, don't you recognize it? What is that Witness? You are that Witness, aren't you?
>
> KEN WILBER,
> *THE SIMPLE FEELING OF BEING*

When trying to get this idea across in class, I will sometimes ask my students if their sense of self, their sense of being *I*, is different from that of other people in the classroom. Invariably they say it is, citing conflicting likes and dislikes to prove their point. I don't doubt that they have a variety of preferences that distinguish each from the other, but that is not what I am asking. "I understand that some of you prefer chocolate ice cream to strawberry, and some of you prefer strawberry to chocolate. What I want to know is this: Is the experience of liking one thing or another different between people? Not the object of our likes and dislikes, but the subjective sense of liking and disliking. Does this differ?"

The answer, we eventually realize, is "no." While the context and content of our life experiences differ, the sense of an *I* having these experiences is the same. There is only one *I* in the universe, and this *I* is the eternal Self, God.

> *One in all, all in One—If only this is realized, no more worry about not being perfect! When Mind and each believing mind are not divided, and undivided are each believing mind and Mind, this is where words fail, for it is not of the past, present, or future.*
>
> SENG-T'SAN, THIRD PATRIARCH OF ZEN

59

This is not so hard to grasp, but often very difficult to accept. We so want to be separate and unique. And we are, just not absolutely.

I am often invited to teach in Aspen, Colorado, and no matter how often I visit, the glory of the aspen tree never fails to stir me to wonder. Aspen trees grow in colonies, each tree sharing a single root system with all the others. A single aspen tree can live from forty to one hundred and fifty years, yet the root system that is its life source can last for tens of thousands of years. Even a forest fire will fail to destroy a colony, for the "eternal self" of the colony is below ground and safe from the devastating heat that burns the trees themselves. After the fire has burned itself out, the colony will regenerate.

Knowing this doesn't in any way minimize the unique beauty or life of any tree in the colony. I have no difficulty distinguishing one tree from another, and simply take delight in looking for and finding subtle differences from tree to tree. And yet none of these trees could live on its own, separate from the root system that feeds it. The trees are an above-ground extension of the underground root system. They are the root system in another form.

What is true of aspens and their root system is true of all living things and God when God is understood from the pantheist point of view. But I am not a pantheist; I am a panentheist: there is something greater than root and tree, something we cannot name because it is not something we can objectify. It is the Witness or the eternal Subject.

Working on this with my students, I projected a classic figure/ground graph onto the large screen in my classroom.

Look at the white space and you see a goblet. Look at the black space and you see the profiles of two people facing one another. This is another way of playing with the metaphors of ocean and wave, and root and tree. But then I ask my students to go a bit deeper and answer the question, "What is the graphic when no one is looking at it?"

RABBI RAMI **GUIDE TO GOD**

The picture isn't one of a goblet or of two profiles. It simply becomes one or the other when you look at it one way or another. But if you aren't looking, what is it? This is the better use of the graphic when speaking about God, the eternal Self, and the *I* that is us all.

It is easy to say, "God is the ocean, we are the waves;" or "God is the root system, we are the trees;" or "God is the ground and we are the figure." But this is not yet the true story. From the panentheist perspective, God embraces and transcends all reality. God isn't yin or yang, but that which embraces them both. God isn't this or that, but this and that and whatever it is that allows this and that to happen in the first place. There is no name for this understanding of God, for, as Lao Tzu reminds us in the first verse of the Chinese Tao te Ching, "The Tao that can be named is not the eternal Tao."

While there are many names of God, there is one that, to my mind, gets at this idea most directly. This is the four letter name of God found in the Hebrew Bible: *Yud–Hey–Vav–Hey*. Unlike most names of God, the Tetragrammaton is not a noun. Jewish tradition forbids Jews from pronouncing the name, and this led to the unfortunate use of a euphemism, *Adonai*, Lord.

62

"Lord" carries lots of baggage (masculine, hierarchical, military), while Y–H–V–H is actually an imperfect form of the Hebrew verb "to be." God is not a being or even a Supreme Being, but being itself. God is the *is-ing* of life, the creative process of birthing and dying, rising and falling. God is both figure and ground, and that process that embraces figuring and grounding.

When we speak of God as a verb, and realize that all life is an expression of God, we realize that life too is a verb. Indeed, there are no things at all, just processes, just happenings. There is nothing fixed and final, there is just this flowing into that and that into this. The impermanence of so-called things reveals that there are no things at all, just temporary happenings that we imagine to be more stable than they really are.

Think of the last time you went to the movies. As you sat mesmerized by the action on the screen, you were oblivious to the fact that all you were watching was a series of still photos flashing before your eyes so quickly as to give you the illusion of continuity. The actors on the screen seemed real because our brains crave and maintain the illusion of continuity. If the film had been slowed down so that there were seconds between each shot, there would have been no story at all. You would quickly have grown bored and left the theater to do something else.

What is true of the movies is true of life. The continuity of self is in your mind. What is actually happening is this moment, and this moment, and this moment, each arising out of a greater field of possibility. Taken separately there is no self at all. But we don't see the world this way. We see continuity and create story. This is the phenomenal ego, the self we experience as *me*, the *I* we imagine is ours alone. The phenomenal ego is as natural as the goblet and the profiles in our figure/ground graphic. It isn't false or evil. It is simply part of the creative *is-ing* that is God.

Most of the time we shift back and forth between figure and ground. We might imagine one is more important than the other, or that one is prior to the other, but this is not so. Figure and ground, goblet and faces, arise together, one highlighting the other depending upon our perspective and focus. For many if not most people, the dance between figure and ground is entertaining enough. We get caught up in the drama, the story, and do all we can to maintain what is essentially an illusory continuity.

So attached are we to continuity that we project

it beyond this life into another: either rebirth in this world or a new life in heaven or hell. Whichever you prefer, the impetus is the same: to maintain the illusion of a separate and eternal self.

Yet there are a few among us who seek to go beyond the illusion of continuity and self. These are the great mystics who dare to draw their attention away from the drama of figure and ground, and ask, Who is it that is watching all this? And when they do the game is up.

But don't imagine that playing the game is wrong. It is natural to us humans. Waking up from the game is no less natural, just a whole lot more rare. It is good to wake up now and then: to know that we aren't just the characters we play or the scripts we read or the drama in which we find ourselves. We are also the creator of all this, the universal Witness, the singular I of awareness that is watching all this as well.

Return to our movie analogy for a moment. The whole point of going to the movies is to get caught up in the film. You have to forget you are staring at a bunch of still photographs flashing before your eyes, otherwise you cannot enjoy the film. But the moment the film ends and the theater lights come up, you know it was a movie. You cease to grieve over the death of a beloved character, and you no longer expect a monster to jump out at you from around the next corner. You can appreciate the movie when you are in the theater and let it go when you leave.

The same is true of your everyday dramas as well. You want to be engaged with life and the people with whom you share it. You want to laugh and cry and even scream in horror when the moment calls for it, but you also need to realize that there is a greater you watching this drama just as you watched the film on the screen. Knowing you are the watcher and the watched allows you to engage life fearlessly and, thus, far more joyously. You are free to feel whatever comes up, and free from the illusion that you are trapped in those feelings.

This freedom is essential to the morality of the Perennial Philosophy, for knowing that you are free to feel even as you are free from these feelings keeps you from acting on those feelings when doing so would cause harm to yourself or others.

CHAPTER FOUR

The Purpose of Life

> *Man's life on earth has only one end and purpose: to identify himself with his eternal Self and so to come to unitive knowledge of the Divine Ground.*
>
> ALDOUS HUXLEY

SO WHO ARE YOU, REALLY? Are you the figure or are you the ground? Or are you that ineffable and unobservable no–thing that is, embracing and transcending both? I suggest you are the latter. But remember, the latter includes the former.

I believe that there is nothing other than God. Everything that is, is a manifestation of God, just as every aspen tree in an aspen grove is an extension of the singular root system that sustains it. So there is no point in seeking God, for God is the seeker. You are looking for yourself, and this is as absurd as trying to bite your own teeth.

Yet most of us operate under an illusion of separateness. We are like an aspen tree that refuses to accept its relationship with the root system and its fellow trees. We are like a wave of an ocean that insists it is other than the ocean, that it is separate from the sea and must find a way to unite with it. There is no way to unite because there is no possibility of separation. There is just the ocean waving.

The same is true with God. Most of us who posit a God insist that we are other than God. And then we invent all kinds of systems of belief to explain that otherness, and all manner of spiritual disciplines to overcome that separateness. Since it is impossible to be other than God, however, we end up working very hard at maintaining the illusion of otherness rather than overcoming it. In fact, the real, if hidden, purpose of religion is to sustain a sense of separateness that we might then be enticed to devote our lives to overcoming.

This is what Zen Buddhism calls "selling water by

the river." If we are thirsty, all we have to do is scoop up some water from the river and drink, but the sellers of water convince us that we can't do that, that only they are allowed to take water, and it is their task to dispense it to us, and that they will be only too happy to do so for a price. That price may be financial, political, or spiritual; it may be loyalty to this or that religion and fealty to this or that religious authority, or it may be a combination of these. Whatever it is, there is always a price.

Before the Law stands a doorkeeper. To this doorkeeper there comes a man from the country who prays for admittance to the Law. But the doorkeeper says that he cannot grant admittance at the moment. The man thinks it over and then asks if he will be allowed in later. "It is possible," says the doorkeeper, "but not at the moment." Since the gate stands open, as usual, and the doorkeeper steps to one side, the man stoops to peer through the gateway into the interior. Observing that, the doorkeeper laughs and

69

says: "If you are so drawn to it, just try to go in despite my veto. But take note: I am powerful. And I am only the least of the doorkeepers. From hall to hall there is one doorkeeper after another, each more powerful than the last. The third doorkeeper is already so terrible that even I cannot bear to look at him." These are difficulties the man from the country has not expected; the Law, he thinks, should surely be accessible at all times and to everyone, but as he now takes a closer look at the doorkeeper in his fur coat, with his big sharp nose and long, thin, black Tar-tar beard, he decides that it is better to wait until he gets permission to enter. The doorkeeper gives him a stool and lets him sit down at one side of the door. There he sits for days and years. He makes many attempts to be admitted, and wearies the doorkeeper by his importunity. The doorkeeper frequently has little interviews with him, asking him questions about his home and many other things, but the questions are put indifferently, as great lords put them, and always finish with the statement that he cannot be let in yet. The man, who has furnished himself with many things for his journey, sacrifices all he has, however valuable, to bribe the doorkeeper. The doorkeeper accepts everything, but always with the remark: "I am only taking it to keep you from thinking you have omitted anything." During these many years the man fixes his attention almost continuously on the doorkeeper. He forgets the other doorkeepers, and this first one seems to him the sole obstacle preventing access to the Law. He curses his bad luck in his early years boldly and loudly, later, as he grows old, he only grumbles to himself. He becomes childish, and since in his yearlong contemplation of the doorkeeper he has come to know even the fleas in his fur collar, he begs the fleas as well to help him to change the doorkeeper's mind. At length his eyesight begins to fail, and he does not know whether the world is really darker or whether his eyes are only deceiving him. Yet in his darkness he is now aware of a radiance that streams inextinguishably from the gateway of the Law. Now he has not very long to live. Before he dies, all his experiences in these long years gather themselves in his head to one point, a

question he has not yet asked the doorkeeper.
He waves him nearer, since he can no longer
raise his stiffening body. The doorkeeper has
to bend low towards him, for the difference in
height between them has altered much to the
man's disadvantage. "What do you want to know
now?" asks the doorkeeper; "you are insatiable."
"Everyone strives to reach the Law," says the
man, "so how does it happen that for all these
many years no one but myself has ever begged
for admittance?" The doorkeeper recognizes
that the man has reached his end, and to let his
failing senses catch the words roars in his ear:
"No one else could ever be admitted here, since
this gate was made only for you. I am now going
to shut it."

FRANZ KAFKA, *BEFORE THE LAW*

Yet God is free. And knowing God is freedom.
And this may be the highest price of all. Many of us
don't want to be free. We don't want to know we are
God. Why? Because being God means being free, and

freedom, despite protest to the contrary, may not be what we truly want. It may be that what we really want is to be taken care of by God; to be told what is right and wrong by God's anointed; to be told how to think and what to read; to be told "these are your friends and these are your enemies;" to be told whom to love and whom to marry. It may just be that freedom from external controls is not something we desire, and because of this we are not willing to pay the price of God–realization because that price is freedom.

If this is true, the Perennial Philosophy will always be a minority view. The Perennialist view is that the sole purpose of your life is to realize that you are God. If the cost of that realization demands that you abandon subservience to others and take responsibility for your own freedom, many if not most people will reject the Perennialist view.

Yet it would be a mistake to assume that to accept the Perennial Philosophy means you have to reject your religion. On the contrary, the Perennial Philosophy exists in all religions. It is, at least from the Perennialist perspective, the heart of every religion. True it isn't the surface teaching which insists that each aspen tree is separate unto itself, but rather

73

it is the deeper teachings that reveal these seemingly separate trees are in fact multiple expressions of a singular root system. But it is part of every religion nonetheless.

So you need not abandon one faith for another, or divest yourself from your religion of choice and swear allegiance to the Perennial Philosophy. You only need delve deeper and deeper into the mystical teachings of your own tradition, for they will lead you to where you already are: God.

And this is the reason you were born: to know God as self and other.

This may seem like a good place to end our discussion, but if you have been paying attention you are not yet satisfied, for if the goal of your life is to know you are God and realize your unity with figure and ground and that which embraces them both, you have to ask, "Who is the you that is to know this?"

74

Lest you imagine I am going to lead you through the whole discussion of "Who Am I" again, let me be very clear. The you we are talking about in this last point of Perennial Philosophy isn't the eternal I but the temporal ego. The I behind all I's already knows it is God. It is your egoic self, your personal I, that suffers from the delusion of separation and otherness. It is the egoic self that has to realize its identity with the eternal Self. It is the I lost in the illusion of alienation and otherness that needs to realize its oneness with the eternal I.

Throughout history there are those human beings who have simply known the truth and lived it. They knew that they were unique and temporary expressions of the singular and timeless reality I am calling God, and because they knew this they felt a kinship with all beings and treated them all justly and with compassion. These were the great sages and saints of all traditions, religious and secular, who modeled a life of love.

I and the Father are one.
JESUS IN GOSPEL ACCORDING TO JOHN, 10:30

I am the Truth.

75

MANSUR AL-HALLAJ

Most of us aren't sages, and even fewer of us are saints. We are ordinary people trapped in the delusion of separate selves, doing what we can to find meaning and purpose in life without actually challenging the illusion we have come to cherish as truth. Assuming we even want to, how do we see through the illusion to the unitive and nondual reality?

This would be a poor guide to God if it ended without offering you a way to actually experience the God we have been talking about. And while I could simply send you out to find the Perennial Philosophy in one established religion or another, I feel I would be cheating you and cheapening the Perennial Philosophy if I didn't do more. There is a perennial spiritual practice—perennial in the sense that it is found in all religions throughout history, and not in the sense that it is endorsed by some official body of Perennial Philosophers that, thankfully, has never existed. It is a simple practice, and one that has occupied me for over thirty years. It is called by different names in different traditions, but it is most widely known by its Sanskrit name: *mantra*.

CHAPTER FIVE

Realizing God Through Mantra

THIS CHAPTER IS VERY SHORT because the practice I wish to share is very easy. It consists of three steps. First, find a mantra that speaks to you. Second, set aside time each day to formally repeat the mantra, either silently or out loud. Third, continue the repetition throughout the day.

FINDING YOUR MANTRA

A *mantra* is a word or phrase that is repeated consciously and with attention. In Hinduism the practice of reciting a mantra is called *japa yoga*, the yoga of repetition. In Judaism it is called *hagah*, cooing like a dove. What the practice is called and what words are repeated depend on the tradition a mantra practice comes from. Every religion has its own version of mantra repetition, and you may wish to explore religions to find the word or phrase that speaks to you.

Many people who take up mantra practice are given a mantra by their guru or teacher. This is how I received my first mantra—now long forgotten—when I took up Transcendental Meditation in 1969, and it's how I received my newest mantra when I was initiated into the Ramakrishna Order of Advaita Vendanta by Swami Swahananda in 2010. But the mantra I use most often came to me through my own reading.

I love the poem "Dude'le" by the eighteenth-century Hasidic rabbi, Levi Yitzchak:

> *Where can I find You—and where can I*
> *not find You?*
> *Above—only You*
> *Below—only You*
> *To the East—only You*
> *To the West—only You*
> *To the South—only You*
> *To the North—only You*
> *If it is good—it is You*
> *If it is not—also You*
> *It is You; It is only You.*

While learning more about the author, I discovered that Levi Yitzchak practiced his own version of mantra yoga by reciting the Hebrew *HaRachaman* (The Compassionate One) over and over without ceasing. This became my root mantra.

> *Hare Krishna Hare Krishna; Krishna Krishna Hare Hare*
> *Hare Rama Hare Rama; Rama Rama Hare Hare*
> (While there are many ways to understand this mantra, I find it helpful to note that *Krishna* and *Rama* are thought to be manifestations of *Vishnu,* the divine power that removes illusions, and the word "Hare," which means "Hail to" or "Welcome," is bidding salutations to these deities. Hindu.)

> *Om Namah Shivaya*
> (Adoration to *Shiva*, the attribute of God representing transformation. Sanskrit scripture.)

> *Namu Amida Butsu*
> ("I take refuge in the Buddha of Infinite Light." This is the Japanese pronunciation of the central mantra of Pure Land Buddhism.)

Om Mani Padme Hum

(While often translated as "Jewel in the Lotus," the Tibetan understanding takes each syllable to mean one of the six *Paramitas* or core virtues of Buddhist living: *Om*/generosity, *Ma*/Morality, *Ni*/Patience, *Pad*/Diligence, *Me*/Renunciation, *Hum*/Wisdom. Tibetan Buddhist.)

Lord Jesus Christ, Son of God, have mercy on me, a sinner (Christian.)

Maranatha

("Come Lord." Christian.)

Sa Ta Na Ma

("Infinity, Birth, Death, Rebirth." Sikh.)

Allah Hu

("God is!" Islam.)

FORMAL PRACTICE

By formal practice I mean setting aside time each day to practice mantra yoga. All you need do is sit in a comfortable upright position, either cross–legged on cushions or in a chair with your feet flat on the floor, close your eyes, and recite. As I said, I have a host of mantras that I recite, some of which can only be given by a guru or rabbi. Rather than share my personal practice, let me share by way of example the mantra practice I learned from the Sikh tradition. While I do not do this specific practice every day, I do use it often and can attest to the fact that it is a highly effective means for becoming aware of the *I* that is God.

When you are ready to practice, sit comfortably with your eyes closed. The mantra we will use here consists of four Sanskrit words: *Sa*, *Ta*, *Na*, *Ma*. These are said to translate into Infinity, Birth, Death, and Rebirth, respectively. Chant each syllable and extend the "a" so that it sounds like *Saaaah, Taaaah, Naaaah, Maaaah*.

The recitation is accompanied by tapping the fingers of each hand to the thumb of that hand: touch the index finger to the thumb with *Sa*; touch the middle finger to the thumb with *Ta*; touch the ring finger to the thumb with Na; and touch the little finger to the thumb with *Ma*.

Repeat this over and over for twelve minutes: chant out loud for two minutes; chant in a whisper for two minutes; chant in silence for four minutes; chant in a whisper for two minutes; and chant out loud for two minutes. That's it.

Can you really realize God in twelve minutes? Why not? You are already God. How long does it take you to realize that the rope coiled in the corner of the garage is a rope and not a snake? How long does it take for you realize that a wave is not and cannot be other than the ocean in which it waves?

OK, maybe it will take you thirteen minutes. My point is that you already know the truth, now you want to manifest it. This will take as long as it takes. The truth is already true, so there is no rush. Just sit and chant.

But let me tell you this: the more you do this, the more loving you become. That is the gift of mantra practice. The more you practice mantra yoga, regardless of the words or phrase you use or the tradition from which they come, there is something about recitation that opens the heart. Which is why you do not want to limit yourself to formal practice only, but want to practice informally throughout the day.

INFORMAL PRACTICE

My informal practice of mantra yoga is based on Levi Yitzchak's mantra, *HaRachaman* (the Compassionate One). I recite this over and again throughout the day. Whenever I find myself with nothing to do—standing in a line for one reason or another, waiting for a meeting to begin or a class to start or an elevator to arrive, I recite *HaRachaman* silently. I have been doing this particular version of mantra yoga for more than fifteen years. It is so ingrained in my psyche that as soon as I shift my attention to it I find my body relaxing, my breath deepening, my heart rate slowing, and my mind expanding in such a manner as to awaken me to a feeling of compassion for and from all things.

I am no saint, and I do not pretend to be one. There are times when I am so stressed that I forget the power of my mantra to undo the stress and negativity. There are times when fear and anger get the better of me. But I find that even then—once I realize what is happening—I can free myself from these negative emotions by chanting *HaRachaman*.

What I promise you is this: if you devote formal time to mantra yoga, and integrate the practice informally into your day as well, over time—far less time than you might think—you will be less and less tied to the narrow mind of self, and more and more awake to the spacious mind of Self. And in this way you realize God as the all in all. And with this realization comes a sense of love for and from all life that makes you a vehicle for compassion and peace. The goal of the Perennial Philosophy isn't selfish—there is no separate self. The goal is love: universal, all–encompassing love.

Seven FAQ

A GUIDE OF THIS SORT cannot answer all your questions about God. What it can do, and what I have set out to do, is guide you to my understanding of God. I have offered this theology to thousands of people over the years, and I have responded to thousands of questions regarding it. Seven questions come up over and again, and I will close the *Rabbi Rami Guide to God* with my brief responses to these questions.

1 *If God is everything, is God evil as well as good? And if God isn't evil, where does evil come from?* Let me start with some basic assumptions. First, good and evil can only be understood in relation to one another. We cannot know good without knowing evil, and we cannot know evil without knowing good. Second, good and evil only exist in

the human dimension.

When trying to demonstrate the first premise, I use the example of a magnet. When working with young people on this idea I hand out thin bar magnets and pairs of safety scissors. I demonstrate the two poles of the magnet, one positive and one negative, and label the positive "good" and the negative "evil." Since evil is something we say we want to avoid, let's cut it out altogether by cutting off the negative pole of the magnet. What happens when we do? The piece we remove develops a positive pole to match its negative pole, and the larger piece we sought to free from negativity simply manifests another negative pole.

Perhaps we didn't cut off enough. So we try again, but the same thing happens. No matter how small we make our magnet, positive and negative remain. Just so with God: you cannot reduce God, that ineffable reality that is both the one and the many, to good or evil.

Why does God manifest both good and evil? For the same reason the magnet manifests both positive and negative poles. Manifesting opposites is what it is to be God. Asking if God is good or evil is like asking of a magnet, is it positive or negative? It is both or it is nothing. For God to be God, God must be everything. Anything less isn't God.

Does this mean that life is both good and evil? No, it means that we humans are both good and evil. Which brings us to my second premise: good and evil make sense only in the context of human behavior.

Tsunamis aren't evil, earthquakes aren't evil, hurricanes aren't evil. They are all the necessary by–products of the way nature functions. Similarly, when the lioness hunts and kills the gazelle, she is not doing something evil. She is simply abiding by the rules of nature. Evil only makes sense when we are talking about human beings.

Natural disasters aren't evil, but when people take advantage of natural disasters to exploit one another, that is evil. When humans demonize one another and use that demonization to excuse acts of cruelty and even genocide against the other; that is evil. When humans exploit nature, torment and torture animals and fellow humans; that is evil. Humans are the only beings on planet Earth who can access their dark side.

The extent to which people identify with the narrow self, the egoic self, the seemingly isolated and alienated self, is the extent to which we perceive the world as a zero-sum game. A zero–sum game is one in which winning requires losing: if I am to win, you must lose; if my team is to win, the other team must lose; if my gender, tribe, country, race, ethnic group, religion is to win, the others must lose.

A zero–sum world is a world at war with itself. It is a world dominated by fear and mistrust. Zero-sum people are always looking over their shoulders knowing that others are seeking to take advantage of them just as they are seeking to take advantage of others. What little if any trust exists in a zero–sum world, relies on ever-changing allegiances that themselves cannot be trusted.

Zero–sum people are frightened, exhausted, angry, and often violent. Their world makes the very idea of compassion absurd. Evil—exploiting the Other, both human and nonhuman—is the inevitable outcome of living in a zero–sum world of competing selves.

The extent to which we realize our unity with all life in, with, and as God determines how free we are from the fear and insanity of zero-sum living, and how free we are to live generously and with compassion. In a nonzero–sum world, there is always enough if we are willing to take care of one another. In a nonzero–sum world, there are those who win more and those who win less, but there are no losers: no one reduced to abject poverty, no one forced into slavery, no one trafficked for another's pleasure, no one exploited or abused.

We move toward evil when we move away from God–realization; we move toward good when we move toward God–realization.

Hell is a huge banquet with everyone sitting at a table six feet wide and infinitely long. The finest foods are offered and only one rule is enforced: you must use the utensils provided. These utensils, too, are six feet long, and feeding oneself with them is impossible: our arms just aren't long enough. Heaven is the same banquet with the same rules. The only difference is this: in Hell people try to feed themselves, in Heaven they have learned to feed one another. In Hell everyone starves. In Heaven all are full.

JEWISH LEGEND

2 If God is everything, and I am God, what happens to me when I die? When it comes to death there are three basic options: (1) you die and everything that was you is you no longer; (2) your body dies but your personality continues in some nonmaterial heaven or hell; or (3) your body dies and your personality continues in a new body. What each of these has in common with the others is the notion that you exist separate from the whole, and that the you that matters is the finite you of the egoic self. Even people who speak of souls and eternal reward and punishment imagine the soul to be an extension of the personality. Otherwise reward and punishment makes no sense. If when I die I am not the person I was when alive, in what sense can I be held responsible for the actions of that now dead self? Why should I be punished or rewarded for what that self did if that self isn't me?

Similarly with reincarnation: people talk about "my past lives" and "my future lives" as if there was an *I* that lives over and over again. Both scenarios, heaven/hell and reincarnation, seem far too egoic for me. They, as well as the notion that you die and that is all there is to it, focus on the temporal self. I prefer a fourth option based on the Perennial Philosophy and the notion that there is another Self, the universal Self, God.

When I share this option with kids, I give them each a piece of rope about eight inches long. I ask them to tie a knot in the rope, and we explore the relationship between the knot and the rope. Clearly the knot is different from the rest of the rope, but just as clearly it isn't other than that rope. You can point to the knot but you cannot remove the knot from the rope that comprises it.

I invite the kids to call this knot by the name of a loved one who has died: a grandparent or a pet, whatever is appropriate. I then have them tie a second knot on the rope. This knot is given the child's name. For simplicity's sake, let's call the first knot Fanny, my grandmother's name, and the second we'll call Rami. Fanny and Rami are not the same. They have different shapes, one may be tighter or looser than the other, one is a bit older than the other. You can clearly differentiate Fanny from Rami. And yet both are the rope and equally so.

Now let's assume that Fanny has died, so we untie her knot. Where does she go? The form is gone, there is no mistaking that, but the rope is no less for that.

91

The rope hasn't changed, and yet Fanny is no longer. That knot is gone forever. Even if I tie another knot in the rope it isn't the same as the one I untied.

The extent to which I loved Fanny, her shape, her smell, her voice, her presence, her stories, etc., is the extent to which I grieve her passing. And no matter how many other knots I tie in that rope, I will still miss Fanny just as much. But missing and being separate from are two different things.

If I limit Fanny to her form, she is gone forever. If I realize she is also the rope, she never left or leaves. So I can mourn the loss of form and still feel connected to the essence, since the essence is God.

I believe that when we die, the form of self ends, but the formless Self that is all selves continues.

> *I died a mineral, and became a plant. I died a plant and rose an animal. I died an animal and I was man. Why should I fear? When was I less by dying?*
>
> RUMI

Before I leave this question, let me offer one more that often arises in response to it: *But what about past life experiences, past life remembrances? How do you explain little children who remember past lives?* The only problem I have with past lives is the notion of ownership. The rope knots and unknots forever. Isn't it possible that the experiences of one knot, being the experiences of the rope itself, are available to other knots, being the same rope?

While I cannot prove my theory, I believe it is possible that the whole retains the experiences of its parts. And if this is so, might it not be possible that some of us, being more sensitive to the whole than others, perceive those experiences either as memories, channeled insights, or telepathic messages? And if they do, some might realize these are from the whole while others, perhaps less sensitive, might mistakenly imagine these experiences belong to them in particular?

Again, I cannot prove this. Nor does it matter to me a whole lot. I am not concerned with past lives or future lives. I am only concerned with living this life with as must compassion and justice as possible. And to do that I believe God–realization is essential.

3If God isn't the Rewarding and Punishing God of the theists, why should I bother with God at all? God matters because God is reality. Understanding reality maximizes your happiness and your capacity for love and compassion. Believing in the theistic notion of a punishing God puts me in the impossible position of having to know which God is the true God whom I must worship to avoid being punished. Since this is impossible to know, believing in one God or another is a matter of faith. Or, to put it more crassly, a crap shoot. Why is your faith in Jesus more true that another's faith in Allah or Krishna? You can only argue for the rightness of your faith choice by appealing to those texts and teachings from that faith choice, and this circular reasoning proves nothing. So no matter how strong your faith, if you think about it rationally, which few really do, you would have to say that your faith is rooted in nothing more than your hope that it is the true faith.

This is not a game I enjoy playing. There is reward and punishment, but it isn't doled out based on faith choice. You are "rewarded" with fearless joy, love, compassion, and peace when you engage in practices that open the narrow self of ego to the spacious self of God. You are "rewarded" with fear, anger, jealousy, and violence when you engage in practices and beliefs that promote the narrow self and its sense of isolation, alienation, and zero-sum worldview.

4 *Why did God create the world?* I don't think there is a "why." I think God is creativity. God is a verb, the Y–H–V–H of the Hebrew Bible, the *is-ing* of the universe. God creates, or, better, manifests or extends for the same reason the sun shines. The sun shines because that is what it is to be a sun. God creates because that is what it is to be God. Does God have a plan for creation? No. God simply creates. Over time creation may evolve to the point that some beings can realize the true nature of reality as God, but this is neither inevitable nor God's aim. God has no aim other than to be God. And being God means creatively manifesting—birthing, growing, dying, and rebirthing over and over.

95

5 *How does evolution and Intelligent Design fit with your understanding of God?* If by evolution you mean the creative process of complex life forms evolving from less complex life forms,

I would simply say this is how God operates in the natural world that you and I can explore scientifically. My problem with Intelligent Design is that it posits a Designer outside reality, someone or something separate from creation, and this I cannot accept.

6 *If I am God, what is the purpose of prayer and communal worship? Am I simply praying to myself?* There are four types of prayer: petition, intercession, adoration, and contemplation. Petition is asking God for something for yourself. Intercession is asking God for something for others. Adoration is an act of praise and devotion to God. Contemplation is cultivating a state of awareness in which the narrow self opens to the spacious Self and knows itself to be that. While I would not discount or dismiss the first three, my own focus is on the fourth. The practice of mantra yoga may be linked to a personal image of God as Krishna or Christ, but for me there is no image, only the experience of compassion that arises when I repeat one of the several mantras with which I have been entrusted.

> *If you have God in mind, simply and solely God, in all things, and carry God into all you do . . . you become one with God in every thought. Just as no diversity stands outside God's unity, so nothing can dissipate the Self you know yourself to be.*
>
> MEISTER ECKHART

Gathering for communal prayer, however, may be something else altogether. I believe there is intrinsic value when a community gathers to affirm its highest values, values rooted not in the xenophobia of selves locked into a zero-sum worldview, but values rooted in the interdependence of all things in, with, and as the One God of which the awakened Self is aware. Just hearing these virtues expounded, whether addressed to a God or not, is of value in that it reminds us of the best of which we are capable. If we gather to promote a jingoistic faith, a zero-sum faith of self-proclaimed winners taking pleasure in not being losers, then I find this not only Self defeating, but self and selfish promoting. I prefer gathering to support one another's efforts to realize God as our true Self, not to reward one another for picking the "true" faith.

97

RABBI RAMI **GUIDE TO GOD**

7If God is everything, and we are God, how can there possibly be a path to God at all? Krishnamurti, one of the greatest spiritual teachers of the twentieth century, said, "Truth is a pathless land." I believe this to be true. There are two ways to understand this statement. First, you could say that Truth is a pathless land because there is no way to it. Truth that can be reduced to the by-product of some methodology isn't the capital "T" truth we are looking for. Truth must transcend the systems we create to entrap it.

The second way one might understand Krishna-ji's teaching is this: Truth is a pathless land because you are always and already in the midst of it. There is no path to *here*, only to *there*. If Truth is *here*, there is no way to get *there*, for there is no *there* to get to.

> *How shall I grasp It? Do not grasp it. That which remains when there is no more grasping is the Self.*
>
> PANCHADASI

I think both understandings are correct. There is no map to Truth and nowhere to go to find it. The

Hebrew Bible, for example, seems to agree with Krishna-ji when Moses says, *lo b'shamayyim he* (It is not in heaven):

> Surely this teaching that I impart to you today isn't too difficult for you, nor is it beyond your grasp. It isn't in the sky, so don't complain, "Who can go up to heaven for us, and get it for us so that we may observe it?" Nor is it across the ocean that you should cry out, "Who can cross the ocean for us and get it for us so that we may observe it?" No, the truth is very close to you; it is in your mouth and in your heart; observe it!" (DEUTERONOMY 30:11–14)

And Jesus, too, carries on this Jewish teaching:

> Jesus said, If your teachers say, "The kingdom is in the sky," the birds of heaven will get it before you do. If they say, "It is in the sea," then the fish will receive it before you do. Rather the kingdom is inside you and outside you. If you know yourselves, then you will be known, and you will know that you are children of the living Father. But if you do not know

yourselves, then you are in poverty and you
are poverty. (JESUS, GOSPEL OF THOMAS, LOGIA 3)

Moses says the Truth is within you that you may live it. Jesus says the kingdom, the way of life that arises when you grasp the Truth is everywhere where the Truth is known. There is nowhere to go, and no one else to be, to grasp and live the Truth.

> *How does a person achieve harmony with the Tao?*
> *Asking the question itself generates disharmony.*
>
> SHIH-T'OU

Yet knowing that there is no way to Truth does not mean there is no path to truths. That is to say, while the absolute may be just beyond and always within our grasp, this doesn't preclude us from exploring the relative truths that point toward it. The world's religions, when read from the Perennial perspective are just such paths. When we walk them well, we discover there is nowhere to go and no one else to be. We discover that what we are called upon to do is live out the compassion and love that naturally arise when we grasp the Truth within and without.

Where do we start? Each of us must start where we are. That may mean with the religion into which we were born, or to the faith to which we are drawn. Or it may mean something more.

In the legend of the Holy Grail each knight must enter the forest in search of the Cup, and each does so at the place that is darkest for him. The forest is a pathless land, and those who enter are going to have to make their own way. But more than that, this particular forest represents the darkest place, the place you are the most broken and wounded and lost.

> The Sufi saint Nasrudin, is crawling on his hands and knees around a brightly lighted street lamp looking for his keys. A friend walks by and joins in the search. Finding nothing, the friend asks, "Where exactly did you drop them?" "In my house," Nasrudin replies. "Then why are we searching out here?" "The light is better out here!" says Nasrudin.

101

Each of the world's religions has its own dark place of entry. For example, for the Buddhist it is grasping; for the Hindu it is illusion; for the Taoist it is imbalance; for the Muslim it is pride; for the Jew it is alienation; and for the Christian it is sin. It may be that you resonate with one or more of these. Or it may be that your darkest place is something else, perhaps something another religion speaks to, or perhaps something best addressed in some other nonreligious manner. Whatever it is, it is there you must begin.

Beginning from the darkest place means beginning from the place of not knowing. It is a place of humbling. It may be a place in which you feel frightened, or alone, or broken, or all three. Whatever it is, it is the place where awakening and healing begins. If you are going to find God, if you are going to discover that you are a manifestation of God, this is the place of entry. If you fail to enter the dark place, you can never heal. And this is the poverty of which Jesus spoke.

For me that poverty and dark place is the narrow self ignorant of the spacious Self of which it is a part. Imagining ourselves apart from rather than a part of God and the natural world God manifests, we live loveless and fearful lives. The entire intent of this guide is to point a way through the darkness and poverty toward light and abundance without assuming the one is God and the other isn't. I may or may not have succeeded. But I did my best, and I can do no better.

ABOUT THE
AUTHOR

BORN YIRACHMIEL BEN YISROEL V'SARAH in 1951, Rami spent several years in kindergarten trying to learn to pronounce his name. Being the only first grader who had to shave, Rami was promoted through school quickly, earning both rabbinic ordination and a Ph.D. Forced to get a job at age thirty, Rami led a congregation for twenty years where he learned that irony, humor, and iconoclasm made for poor bedside manner, and honesty was rarely the best policy when it came to religion. Author of over two dozen books and hundreds of essays, Rami writes a regular column for *Spirituality & Health* magazine entitled "Roadside Assistance for the Spiritual Traveler."